# 30 ways to win a bid

**Anna Hutton-North**
**www.sabreassociates.co.uk**

ISBN: 978-0-244-62588-7

Edition: 0517_1

# Contents

"The old adage with advertising is that the 50% is wasted is an unknown.

This should never be the case with bids and proposals."

 # Why be effective at bidding?

Bids are the life-blood of any business-to-business organisation. Without them there is no inflow of new business or retention of existing custom.

Although the term 'bid' is referred to within this book, it is interchangeable and is used in an all-encompassing way to include RFI, ITN, ITT, tender, proposal, pitch, opportunity, presentation etc. The terminology may differ, depending upon the industry you operate in, but the approach and practice is the same.

In the same way the reference to 'bid team' is used and applies to any individual or team who are producing bids or proposals, even if their job title isn't explicitly 'bids'.

Within the UK there are no reliable records of the total value of the bids and tenders let each year, the closest available publically are the published public sector figures. Using these as a base line we can safely assume there are over 100,000 tenders let and won each year, worth a total value of over £700 billion. Interestingly these figures have grown over the past five years despite Brexit and the ongoing economic uncertainty.

However organisations are finding competition tougher. Although the number of bids are growing there is an increasing number which are for a lower value or which are being combined. Both of these make work winning more difficult for organisations. This is a major shift for organisations. No longer can the bid team be seen as an isolated unit. It needs to be an integral part of the client-facing team.

Increasing competition means that the effort and resource to win bids needs to be far more focused. That means having a clear bid-to-win approach, which runs through the whole organisation.

The move towards combined tenders provides a streamlined approach for larger organisations, not needing to submit multiple lots within a single contract. However for the SME this can reduce or even eliminate the opportunities of bidding for work. The response to this is to be part of a supply chain or look to partner with complimentary organisations, although profit margins may be effected.

The bid market is fluid; it reaches across multi-industries, often with complex organisations, each of whom are developing and adapting to a changing environment.

For this reason the organisation bidding for work not only needs to be continually raising the bar in terms of bidding to win, but also in keeping up to date with clients, markets and trends.

Anyone involved in bids or work winning knows that there is no single answer to making sure you have the winning bid. Instead it is a number of smaller variables, each of which needs to be individually tweaked and adapted for each new client. Although there needs to consistency this should not become vanilla. Each bid needs its own energy and spark to produce a compelling solution for the client.

That means bidding for work can become incredibly complex and time consuming, resulting in bid teams looking to cut corners or find ways round what are viewed as over onerous bid processes and procedures. This doesn't help the bid overall. Bid processes and procedures are created for a reason; they provide structure, rigour and transparency across the organisation. They do however need to be flexible enough to adapt with the organisation and its bidding needs.

This book is designed to equip the an organisation with an effective way to bid for work, creating a bid team with the skills to create meaningful bids that will gel with the client and help the organisation to win more work. After all – the only reason to bid for work is to win the work.

 # Recognising what a bid is

There is one underlying theme throughout this book: *'the bid is far more than just the document'*. For many bid professionals this is an accepted given; however there are still regular examples in offices up and down the country where the mention of a bid makes teams open up bid templates and start thinking about colours, layouts and display. This is not the answer to a successful bid.

Instead the Director responsible for the company's bids and proposals will recognise that the bid starts long before a tender document is produced. It is the evaluation of an opportunity, to prospect, to bid which means that the bid is the responsibility of the whole client facing team.

In essence there are five key steps within any bid. These are:

- Market analysis
- Targets and segmentation
- Identifying opportunities
- Pursuits and proposals (including producing the bid)
- Client management and feedback

These five stages are inter-related, as can be seen in Figure 1: The stages of the bid lifecycle.

## *Figure 1 - The five stages of a bid lifecycle*

Client review

Pursuit &
proposals

Market
analysis

Identify
opportunities

Targets &
segmentation

These stages need to be embedded within the organisation, so that the whole client facing team is focusing on the bid opportunity. Understanding these five stages of the bid lifecycle is the critical element. By recognising the bid lifecycle in its entirety, the organisation starts to have a greater empathy with the bid itself and that in turn gives the organisation a greater chance of success.

# Introducing the five stages of a bid lifecycle

The reason there are five stages is to highlight that a bid does not start when a bid notice is sent out. Anyone who is relying merely on electronic notification of bids is setting the company to fail. The client facing team needs to begin work on the opportunity way before a notification or announcement is made.

After all, the bid is merely part of the ongoing spectrum of the work winning and delivery agenda, as shown in Figure 2.

*Figure 2 – Where bids fit into the work winning spectrum*

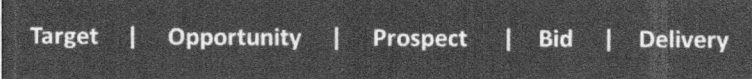

In order to be able to turn the organisation into a client-centric business, the client-facing teams need to have cohesion and compatibility across five tenements; these are:
- The right skill levels to ensure they can adequately fulfil their role within the five stages.
- The organisation has achieved the right level of client engagement at each step along the work winning spectrum and that individual teams are contributing to retaining or growing client engagement seamlessly so the client has an uninterrupted journey.
- Having access to the data to input and extract at the point required during the bid life cycle.
- Having sight of, and understand the importance of the key targets whether by company, by individual or by key account.

- Understand the processes that flow across the work winning spectrum and recognise where input and ownership is required.

The five tenements required for a work winning culture are shown in Figure 3.

*Figure 3 – The five tenements*

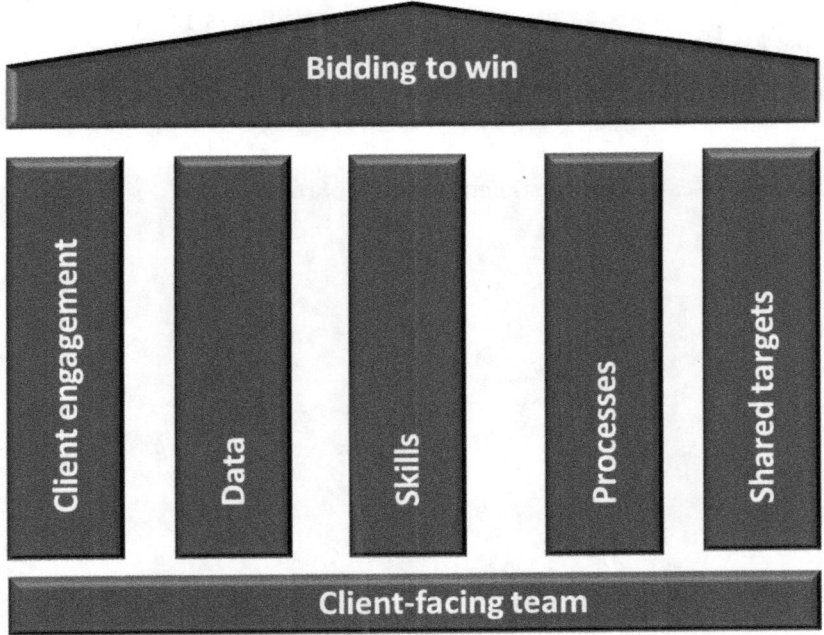

Integrating the five tenements can be done in a variety of ways. The key element is to effectively integrate the bid function into the client-facing team.

This can be achieved by giving business development teams responsibility for producing their own proposals or by having both bids and marketing/sales reporting into one Director so there is a shared approach, goal and ethos.

Some organisations decide to have a central bid team while others have devolved responsibility within the business teams.

There should be one shared strategy and vision across all the client-facing teams. To achieve real integration they need to have one set of goals, shared targets and clear responsibilities for sharing and developing the opportunity through its lifecycle. Figure 4 shows how client opportunities need to be at the centre of everything.

*Figure 4 – Establishing a client-facing approach*

Whatever organisational approach is taken in setting up the bid function the over-riding concept needs to be one of a united client-facing team that is able to target, approach and win work seamlessly as one team.

 **Market Analysis**

"Understanding the marketplace means that the opportunities being pursued will be those which are the best fit with the business' services or products."

# What are you offering

How can customers buy from you if they don't know what you sell? It is an age-old adage but one that is fundamental to winning work.

In order to raise awareness of your organisation's products or services they have to first be clearly articulated. The articulation needs to be carefully crafted though; it usually will be either technically-rich or issue-based that resonate with a client's problem. It is never a list of features.

To establish what you are offering carry out a short review that identifies:

- Every product or service that you offer. Create an overall list so that you can clearly see every offering available.
- Look at the product or service descriptions and see if they resonate with the reasons clients declare that they buy. Check that you are not listing features when the client is looking for solutions to issues.
- Look at the overall list and decide if it is potentially too long or too confusing. Where possible bring services together to provide overall solutions to a client's issues to create families of offering.
- Look at the inter-relations of the list to identify if there are natural value-add sales or next-step purchases. Pull these together so that they can be included as cross-selling opportunities within the client action plans.

When you are carrying out the review use a detached viewpoint, look at the services from a client's perspective. This will resonate with the client and thus give you greater traction. It also makes your offering more attractive to the client as you can demonstrate how the products and services provide a solution to the problem. Grouping products together allows you to do multiple sales through one interaction, facilitating cross-selling and up-selling either through a single proposal or further upstream.

**Checklist:**

- *Be able to articulate your company's offering in a way that responds to the client's triggers for buying.*
- *Group related products and services together to demonstrate integrated solutions, making it easier for cross-selling opportunities.*
- *Build the families of services into the account plans to allow for upstream sales.*

# Make it easy for clients to find out more about you

The relationship with the client needs to start way before the bidding process.

That means you need to be signposting the company and its services at the initial stages of reaching out to them.

Remember there are two key elements to raising your profile: accessible information and signposting.

Clients will want to be able to have an easy-to-understand overview of who the company is, what they provide and why other clients chose you. This needs to be available in a variety of formats that will resonate with your client base.

There are numerous digital, print and personal channels, whether it is a website, newsletters, Twitter feeds, Linked In discussion groups, What'sApp forums, presentations, seminars or one-to-one meetings.

Decide which channels will be most beneficial to you and build a strong presence that succinctly encapsulates the company so that clients have a clear view on what you can provide ahead of any bid.

Once these channels are established, the important step is to clearly signpost them. Identify the best way of introducing them to your targets and clients, whether it is through digital invites, emails, formal letters, brochures or even through your business cards.

Building up a virtual and physical rapport will create a familiarity ahead of a bid.

**Checklist:**

- *Select the most beneficial channels for your clients.*
- *Have a clear plan on how you will signpost critical company information.*

# Be consistent with how you portray the company and what it offers

No bid document is ever read in isolation. There is either a prior awareness or a subsequent cross-checking.

This means that to ensure what you have included within your bid is seen as credible, it must be consistent with everything else you are saying.

There needs to be a consistency across all your channels, including your bid documentation, whether the channel is digital, print or personal.

All bid documents need to be tailored to bring out the most relevant experience; therefore the wording is not going to be exactly the same. However there should be a similarity to show credible experience. It is a useful exercise to check that relevant experience, service/products and recent client stories are being shared between the bid library, the website and client presentations.

**Checklist:**

- *Carry out an audit of how the company is portrayed to ensure consistency.*
- *Make sure you are using case studies consistently across all your channels including your bid library.*

## 4    Establish a clear bid process

Having a clear bid process as part of the five tenements is not a suggestion for a rigid bureaucratic formula. Rather it is about the bid team working with the rest of the client-facing teams so that there is one integrated approach to handling bids and opportunities.

Part of this exercise is a cultural education step, so that client-facing managers and Directors are sharing information on potential up-coming opportunities with the bid team rather than simply waiting and then requesting a bid document to be produced.

Best practice around this includes sharing client updates, actively updating the bid team prior to a bid, working together to create a bid-winning strategy and completing a bid through to feedback and debrief.

Checklist:

- Each organisation will have their own personal approach to their bid process however the key milestones are:
    - What to bid
    - How to bid
    - How to create a winning bid
- Be able to articulate what the bid process is within a document which can be shared.

- Educate, where necessary, the wider organisation as to what the bid process is, and the value of working together.

## Case study: Considering the complexities of a consortium bid

When a large public sector IT bid was let, a consortium of main service provider and three specialist niche suppliers joined together to create a consortium bid.

The issue was how the bid could take into account the four partners' different inputs, offerings and examples so that the client had a clear understanding on what the consortium's solution was, how it differentiated itself from its competitors and how the partnership would work together to deliver the solution.

The solution was to appoint an independent Bid Director to manage this major bid. The Bid Director was able to bring the four partners together and identify the bid winning strategy. As well as helping to co-ordinate the bid document requirements, they were able to edit the final response to ensure there was a clear solution and prepare the team for the client presentation.

By having an independent Bid Director, it meant the respective partners were able to focus on delivering the technical aspects of the bid rather than having to manage and coordinate the overarching bid programme, which meant a cohesive, compelling bid that ran to schedule and was delivered on time.

30 ways to win a bid

 **Targets and segmentation**

"Having business development and bids working closely together means the organisation can target its bid activities far more effectively."

# 5     Know your clients

Each bid benefits from a personalised approach. By having an understanding of the client from the other parts of the client-facing teams who are already interacting with them and their organisation, it is possible to decide on the most effective way of preparing the bid.

Questions to consider include:

- Should the approach be formal or informal - so that the tone and language used are suitable.
- Who are the key decision makers, and what are their burning issues?

Think about how these can be brought out and addressed within the document or presentation.

Also consider how clients would prefer to engage; do they see themselves as techno-savy and innovative – if so think about whether your bid should be an e-based approach; are they traditional needing a conservative approach, or has their procurement team been prescriptive in what needs to be delivered?

**Checklist:**

- *Work with the other client-facing teams to understand the client's issues and problems.*
- *Personalise your bid so that it reflects your understanding of the client and their needs.*
- *Create a summary list to decide the bid approach.*

# 6     Tracking your opportunities

From the perspective of the Director responsible for bids and proposals, it is essential that there is transparent tracking of business opportunities. By forward managing the opportunities it is possible to have a view of which will convert into proposals.

This is important for two reasons:
- Having an awareness of the opportunities with a view to resource allocation for proposal creation.
- Ensuring that the team are gathering information around client needs, burning platforms and potential value propositions ahead of the proposal process.

There are different approaches which can be taken to track the opportunities:
- Using a CRM system where the opportunities are logged and have probability of conversion and potential timings included.
- Regularly shared client team updates.
- Tracking opportunities via sector experts.

Building in pre-bid planning is good practice; however it does require the time to be set up and monitored, something which can be difficult when there are client opportunity deadlines to be met.

**Checklist:**

- *Adjust the business development process to include opportunity tracking.*
- *Identify the best approach for tracking opportunities which gives visibility but is not heavily bureaucratic.*
- *Ensure adequate time is given to acting on advance knowledge of a bid to make the bid more effective.*

# 7    Share client insights

It is important that the bid team all have access to the same information as the rest of the client-facing team.

The information needs to be fresh, timely and relevant. Consideration needs to be given as to how the bid team can tap into the company's collective data pool. It may be through a formal CRM system, client engagement system or client debriefs; alternatively it may be via more informal channels such as emails, team updates or news updates.

Whichever process is employed it needs to be fluid, dynamic and recognised by the organisation. This means that information will flow automatically to the bid team and then be dispersed throughout the team without the need for constant manual-intensive intervention.

Client insights are a valuable tool for the bid team; they allow the bid to be tailored to the main issues the client is facing. References can be made to key credentials which clients are looking for and highlight specific services or key differentials that will help a client to resolve current problems.

**Checklist:**

- *Identify how client insights from across the whole organisation can flow into the bid team.*
- *Consider how client insights can be used effectively within the bid to provide real perspicuity.*

# Case study: Addressing low win rates

A waste management organisation was suffering from a perpetual low win rate. They needed to address this as the business was suffering from a lack of new business.

The organisation's low win rate for the bids needed to be resolved so that the cost of bidding was reduced and the value of the bids won increased.

Upon investigation it was found that the issue wasn't just about the low win rate, so rather than solely focusing on the bid production, the company decided to address the whole bid life-cycle.

The subsequent analysis showed that work could be done on their targeting process which would both increase opportunities to bid for as well as increasing the value of the bids as well. The second phase was then to look at the actual bid process and subsequent follow up. A number of quick wins were developed which helped to address the previous low win rates.

The overall result was that the bid team worked more effectively with Sales and Marketing to target the opportunities which would provide realistic wins, thus reducing spent-effort and increasing the win rate.

 **Identifying opportunities**

"Having a clear must-win bid strategy
helps to prioritise where the
organisation should focus
its bid efforts and resources."

# 8    Seeing the bid document

The tender has come out, the questions have been allocated and everyone is working on their answer.

Don't forget to share all of the bid documentation though. Ensure everyone working on the bid has visibility of the original document, so they are aware of any stated constraints contained within the requirements. Failure to do so can result in simple mistakes which result in a non-compliant bid, immediately eliminating the company from the tender process.

Make sure that all the questions are reviewed together so that the final submission can be checked for consistency and that the bid complies with the invitation to tender.

**Checklist:**

- *Ensure the bid documents are circulated and available – either on a central resource or sent to individuals.*
- *Be aware of any constraints and ensure the bid is compliant.*

# Think about investing time in research

Bids have a way of becoming all consuming; there rarely feels like any let-up in bid production. However being able to carve out time to carry out client research at the beginning of the bid is invaluable. This research combined with the shared insights from client-facing managers and Directors means that the bid team have a rich awareness of the client's organisation, the issues they face, the personalities to be dealt with and their preferences for interaction.

Research can range from a simple search through a client's website to a more in-depth deep-dive that looks at their annual accounts and CSR statements. If your organisation has a business database identify who their competitors are, and how the competitors are differentiating themselves in the market. Look to see if there are any market research papers on the sector or opinion pieces talking about what companies within their industry will be facing over the next 3-5 years.

**Checklist:**

- *Consider making time to research the client organisation at the beginning of a bid lifecycle.*
- *Share the research findings with the rest of the bid team.*

# 10   Know your win rates

Monitoring success rates is important; every bid team wants to know how well they are doing and monitoring win rates is one way of doing this.

Deciding what to measure is important though; some of the questions to pose are:

How often are you going to measure; is it weekly, monthly or quarterly?
Do you have an easy way of seeing bid submission data, ie is there a central place for finding out how many bids have been submitted and the resulting win/loss, or is the bid team going to have to create a process and repository?
Who needs to see the information? Are bid results included within a monthly sales report, within quarterly client meetings or as part of a Board report? This may also help determine the frequency of the reports required.

A key decision is around what to actually measure to do this effectively; think about the whole bid lifecycle. Are you going to monitor how many opportunities are available, how many are pursued, how many convert to formal tenders, how many are won or lost?

In addition to volume it might be worth considering measuring value as well in order to monitor trends in increasing or decreasing value year on year.

The final consideration is what should be done with the information by the bid team; should there be some type of trend analysis to identify the performance of the team. It is worth identifying whether the data can be interrogated to find lessons learnt that will help the whole client-facing team to continually improve and raise the bar.

**Checklist:**

- *Decide what needs to be measured, how often and who will view the final report.*
- *Identify if the client-facing teams can use the information to continually raise their performance.*

 ## Case study: Why the organisation needs to win – not just the bid team

A real estate organisation was submitting tenders that were scoring well on pricing but not achieving good scores for its quality element. They were consistently coming in second place.

The MD and Commercial Director were keen to get expert help to coach their bid team. The specialist help looked at both how they were approaching the bid and in the way they were responding.

A comprehensive review of the bid process highlighted the difference in approach being adopted by the Operations team and the Commercial team.

It became apparent that there was a mind-set ingrained within the Operations team that did not see any value in changing the way they approached bids. There was a belief that because the bid specialist was not working day-to-day in the real estate arena they could not help with the proposal.

Although the Exec Team saw a need for a change they were unable to implement a cultural change that would bring the whole of the organisation along the transformation journey to put winning bids at the centre of the business.

The Board had recognised the need to change and provided the potential solution, however they failed to take the senior managers with them and embed the changes. This meant that the blockers in the firm ensured the bids continued to be carried out in the same way, resulting in a continuing lack of wins.

For anyone needing to implement major bid changes, it needs to be accompanied by a cultural change programme across the whole client facing team.

30 ways to win a bid

## Pursuit and Proposals

"To create a winning proposal
the organisation needs to have energy,
commitment and passion."

# What's hot and what's not

Working on client accounts, there is usually no shortage of opportunities. However the Director responsible for Business Development and Marketing needs to be working with the bid teams and be thinking about the priority opportunities as part of the overall work winning strategy.

There are different terminologies applied to this process: bid/no bid, go/no go, what's hot/what's not. Whatever term is used the sentiment is the same, it is a gatekeeper that requires you to work with the proposal team to stop and rationalise whether the organisation should be pursuing the opportunity. This means asking questions such as:

- Is there a strong chance of winning?
- Is it an important contract to secure?
- Is it with a key client?
- Is there resource available to effectively pursue?
- Will it generate the required levels of profitability?

To help make the decision over whether the opportunities should be pursued or not, a set of decision questions should be used. These questions should be consistent, as it allows the opportunities to be compared against each other. By evaluating opportunities they can be ranked for priority, allowing the decision to be based on fact rather than just an emotional or gut feel.

The decision making on a bid/no bid process can take a number of forms including:

*Standard Questionnaire:*
A simple questionnaire with Yes/No answers to give an overall Yes/No answer. While this is quick it is limited in terms of prioritisation ranking.

*Weighted Questionnaire:*
A questionnaire where the questions have weightings (ie a score of 1-5), allowing priority to be given to key areas such as:
- Is the bid of strategic importance?
- Is it for a key client?

The advantage of this method is that the final weighting can then be compared against the other opportunities to give the firm a hierarchy of priorities.

*Balanced scorecard:*
Using a balanced scorecard to create four key areas that ensure the opportunity responds to each of them is a more sophisticated approach. The areas can include demonstrable experience, key sector/key client, profit level and resources to deliver. The advantage is that the opportunities can be quantified across a number of measures to establish comparable priorities.

Whichever approach is adopted, it is important that the results are transparent and can be easily compared. This is particularly important when a recommendation of 'non-pursuit' is made.

Dealing with the client team politics and managing the personalities involved within the what's hot/what's not can be fraught. However the process is imperative as a corporate requirement, it focuses the organisation's effort and resources on the time and effort to win strategically important opportunities rather than taking a scattergun approach to try and go after everything.

**Checklist:**

- *Build a what's hot/what's not gateway into your business development process.*
- *Make sure the decision making criteria is robust and seen as relevant by the business so that it is adhered to.*
- *Ensure the results can be easily compared so that the organisation can prioritise the opportunities to pursue.*
- *Ensure there is Executive support for the process to prevent it from becoming a form-filling exercise which is then ignored.*

# 12    Evaluation whether to pitch or not

One of the hardest jobs within the bid team is to evaluate whether to actually bid or not. Opportunities with key clients are obvious bids, however consideration needs to be taken into account on a number of peripheral issues: does the bid team have resource available to bid, does the company actually want that kind of work, does it make financial sense to bid for the work, do you have a realistic chance of winning or are you being used as a price comparator?

The list is not exhaustive – but it is an idea to create a company scorecard that allows the bid team to identify and prioritise the must-have bids and weed out those which don't offer the same attraction.

The decision to bid/no bid should be taken early on, so that time, resource and effort aren't invested into a redundant opportunity. That doesn't mean that a later review should not be carried out if the remit or understanding of the bid changes – making it less attractive.

**Checklist:**

- *Create a bid/no bid scorecard which the bid team can use to prioritise bids.*
- *Obtain Board approval of the process to ensure the bid/no bid decision is adhered to.*

# 13  Who has the final say

Identifying who has the final sign-off of the bid needs to be established by the bid leader at the outset. There are logistical considerations such as: are they around and available when sign off is due; are they aware they are signing off the document; will they have sight of a draft?

All of these then need to be factored in to the bid schedule.

As well as the logistical considerations, the bid leader needs to consider the personality of the person signing off. Their desire to be involved may be tempered by the actual time they have available. If they want to be seen as directly involved but are unable to join the kick-off or review sessions then the bid leader may need to think creatively about their input. Options include organising personal welcome notes to the team; weekly updates being sent by them or ad-hoc catch ups when possible.

The bid leader needs to understand the individual's preference for working. If you have not worked together before, then establishing a working rapport, ascertaining how they want to be updated on bid progress and at which milestones they want to be involved in is important to ensure the bid process runs smoothly.

**Checklist:**

- *Build a rapport and ensure you establish how the person signing off the bid would prefer to be involved.*
- *Confirm what time they have available.*
- *Check which milestones and reviews do they want to be involved in.*

- *Use lateral thinking to get around any potential bottle-necks in bid schedules when key people are known not to be available.*

## 14     Build a bid library or database

It is universally recognised that for maximum impact each bid produced needs to be tailored and personalised. This can be time and resource consuming.

One answer can be to create a central bid library or database that holds key bid data and information.

This is not a way of creating vanilla-style approach bids, rather it is about having building blocks that can be used to create a winning bid.

Bid libraries usually break down into three components: templates, core company information and evolving supporting examples.

The templates include pre-formatted documents such as a bid submission, financial scenarios and pitch presentations.

Core company information is usually fairly static and covers the company's credentials, history and approach around things such as health and safety, financial history, numbers of employees, organograms, corporate social responsibility and environmental commitments, professional associations and institutions, client lists and sector summaries.

Evolving supporting examples should cover information which is continually updated and supplemented. This includes client case studies, overviews of products and services, data technical sheets and team profiles or CVs.

**Checklist:**

- *Look at how bid information can be held and accessed centrally.*
- *Continually update your bid library with new examples of client case studies, team profiles and new products or services.*

## 15     Have a dedicated bids resource

If your company wants to be regularly securing work then don't leave it to the client facing professionals or account managers to have to handle the opportunity alone.

Bid teams have a discrete and specific set of skills that allow them to craft winning bid strategies, manage complex tenders, draft compelling bid submissions and help teams to prepare for the pitch or presentation.

Having a dedicated bids resource means there is a bid professional that can support the client facing team, inputting valuable knowledge on how to establish a winning bid, develop a bid strategy and co-ordinate the bid submission and pitch.

In addition having a dedicated bid resource means that bid libraries and bid presentations are easily to hand.

**Checklist:**

- *Having a dedicated bids resource will provide specialist knowledge on creating winning bid strategies, as well as a time efficiency element to the bids.*
- *Investing in a bids resource will mean the organisation has access to a centralised bid library, templates and processes.*

# 16    Create consistent bids

Creating consistency should not be confused with re-using the same bid over-and-over again. Consistency is about producing a bid in a time-effective manner and being harmonious with all of the other company channels that the client is interacting with.

Consistency can be achieved through a variety of methods; having a central bid library where information can be easily accessed is a prime example. Ensuring all the bid team receive lessons-learnt from previous bids means mistakes will not be replicated and require fixing again. Having a consistent approach means any one of the bid team can fill in if there is a sudden unexpected absence. All of these allow the bid team to be more effective in the way bids are handled and produced.

The tone, content and visual identity of the bid should also be consistent with the company's other channels, such as websites, client updates and data sheets. Not only does this allow the information to be shared more effectively across all the platforms, it also means that clients recognise the offering, its value and point of differentiation wherever their touch-point is.

**Checklist:**

- *Think how you can create consistent bids in a time-effective way.*
- *Ensure your bids are consistent with the other client facing channels.*

# 17     Make the team/solution come alive

The enthusiasm, energy and desire to win permeate the bid; the client is subtly aware of the interest of the bid team in the opportunity.

It manifests itself in the prior conversations and questions around the bid, the tone and wording used in the response and the body language during the presentation.

It can be difficult for the bid leaders to ignite the team, particularly if there are heavy workloads, team members who are unfamiliar with each other, disparate grades or a mundane offering.

This requires the bid leader to "talk the talk and walk the walk" and lead by example. There are some easy fixes such as bringing the team together outside of the bid to help create a feeling of cohesion; promoting the benefits the bid will bring to the organisation or looking to inject creativity through lateral thinking.

The bid leader needs to be able to read the team and pick up on the underlying tensions. Being able to have time with individuals outside of the bid meetings allows the bid leader to centre on how an individual feels and address accordingly.

One technique is to use more vocal team members to become the bid champions, encourage senior members to buddy or mentor junior team members. Let the team have a full-on innovation and creativity session to make the bid really stand out.

**Checklist:**

- *Ascertain the mood of the bid team and work out a strategy of energising and enthusing.*
- *Make sure everyone involved in the bid has a role to play and is passionate about winning.*

# 18    Use technology to support your bids

Technology is always changing and adapting, and provides some exciting opportunities for creating new and compelling bid formats. Options include interactive pdfs, interactive videos, webinars, multi-media productions and websites.

However before embarking on a technology-based bid carry out some basic checks: ensure someone in the organisation, or your supplier, is totally au fait with using the technology.

Bids can become time critical and trying to handle new technology at the same time as completing a bid when the deadline is looming will not necessarily deliver the best results.

It is advisable to check with the client that they can receive and view the technology you propose to use; it is frustrating to produce a winning bid that cannot be viewed by the client because of technical issues.

Even if clients are able to view it is still worth considering a back-up in case there are system issues outside of your control on the day of submission.

One small word of caution: new technology is not the answer for all clients. Make sure you establish the best bid channel for your client before deciding on an e-response.

**Checklist:**

- *Keep abreast of technology so that you are able to match up the best format to your client's interests and needs.*
- *Always have a back-up plan in case the technology fails.*
- *Only use a technology that someone within the bid team is practiced in using.*

## Case study: Helping consultants be bid writers

A consulting house had a central bid team, however it was felt that their experience handling all the bids and proposals, meant their expertise was being used on lower value bids, preventing them from being able to make a difference on the key must-win proposals.

The response was to create an environment that helped their fee earning consultants to be able to produce their own quotations and bids.

This was achieved through a dual-approach: bid writing skills and bid writing support/resources. A skills training/refreshing programme was created that covered elements such as:
- Converting an opportunity to a bid.
- How to manage a bid.
- How to write a bid.

Attention was given to the supporting resources and support that would help consultants create their own bids. This included standard boilerplate text for key areas such as company introduction, HSQ, CSR, T&Cs, organisation structure and company information.

The results were two-fold; the fee earners began to recognise what opportunities would convert to a proposal, and were able to be more effective with their business development function, and the bid team was able to concentrate on adding value to major bids.

 **Producing the bid**

"All the thoughts, energy insights and work to create a compelling proposition have to be distilled in to a single proposal."

 **19**        **Appointing a bid leader**

Something to consider, particularly when handling large or complex bids is appointing someone who will be the bid leader. This is to ensure that there is a bid owner who will be able to establish the tone of the bid, as well as co-ordinate all the necessary resources and inputs required throughout the bid life-cycle.

One of the first actions is usually to establish a meeting to agree the 'what' of the bid. This clearly sets out how the client needs to be addressed and provides succinct messages for the whole team to be aware of.

Secondly they need to ensure there is agreement on 'how' the bid will be delivered. If procurement have been prescriptive then there is little scope for flexibility. However if no set guidelines have been laid down then the team need to identify the most suitable vehicle for getting messages over. This could be a placemat or a poster; whatever you decide make sure that it fits in with the overall bid and provides enough flexibility for your messages.

One aspect which the bid leader needs to apply careful consideration to is the 'who'. It needs to have the right person or team to deliver the bid in a coherent, concise and compelling manner. The bid leader needs to establish who the client is expecting when this decision is finalised. It is also important that only the speakers attend; try to avoid an entourage of 'bag carriers'.

Bid teams usually have bid professionals with varying degrees of experience and confidence. As the bid leader it is important to be alert to who is confident and who needs help; use your skills to help sort them out without knocking their confidence.

When it comes to pitches and presentations the bid leader should be leading the call for run-throughs and practice. Rehearse, rehearse and rehearse again. It gives everyone an opportunity to see what is working well, what needs to be moved around and allows you to fix the glitches well before the final performance.

Being a bid leader is not easy; it can mean some tough decisions. Don't be afraid to swap out a team member if it's not working. The main thing to focus on is a successful bid.

**Checklist:**

- *Appoint a bid leader who can be supportive, decisive and make tough decisions.*
- *Ensure the team listen to the bid leader – they have the best interests of the bid at heart.*
- *The bid leader should not be expected to produce the document particularly on large or complex opportunities.*
- *The right bid leader will exhibit strong people, organisational and leadership skills.*
- *The purpose of the bid leader is to keep the bid on track so that each of the relevant sections is delivered in a timely and consistent manner.*
- *The bid leader should also act as the independent reviewer.*

## 20     Personalise the response for the client

Everyone talks about the importance of personalisation for clients; but personalisation is more than just changing the name on the bid submission.

Bid personalisation should be split into three areas:
• Client's burning platforms and needs
• Sector issues affecting client
• Flexibility of bid materials

Being able to identify the client's burning platforms will allow you to translate these into value propositions, ie the story line that runs through the bid.

Use your answers to demonstrate how you have addressed similar scenarios with other clients, include details of the benefits the clients received as a result and wherever possible put a value on the benefit delivered.

Look at the industry issues and how these are impacting the client's business.  Consider where you have other clients (even if those clients are in other sectors) whose businesses are facing similar situations and where you were able to help or bring a suitable solution.

If there is someone within the organisation who is an industry expert make sure they are involved in the bid opportunity so that they can share their knowledge and thoughts.

The final area is how to present the bid. It is difficult to personalise an electronic submission that uses an e-platform to collect text based responses. Where possible though consider what will help stand out from the competition; that makes your submission memorable and creates a lasting experience for the client. This may be using digital solutions for media companies or tactile handouts for retail clients. It doesn't necessarily need to be whizzy and high-tech. Simple can be effective. It is also possible to get creative with the presentation so that instead of the standard powerpoint the team could use a placemat, portable whiteboards or a short video as a replacement.

**Checklist:**

- *Every bid should be personalised; there is no excuse for simply changing a client's name within a previous bid.*
- *Find out everything you can about the client so that you can tailor the questions to respond to their key issues.*
- *If you have access to an industry expert or industry insights then see what other organisations are doing to address industry issues and weave these into your solution.*
- *Think about how you can create a memorable bid; be creative with the bid document. Include supporting materials which show you have thought about their issues or main culture. It may be branded CDs, accompanying videos or bid packaging. Don't mistake gimmicks for substance though. The supporting items need to add value in their own right.*
- *Using a company's products or services within the bid can be powerful; however if you are including anything of the client*

*brand make sure you are not infringing any copyright. It is also a good idea to ensure there is no negativity associated with the way products or services are employed or deployed.*

## 21    Using the six-step process

When it comes to writing the document there are various considerations, however there is a logical six-step process which can be adapted and refined.

1.  Identify existing responses and copy which can be adapted.
2.  Obtain operations/delivery input particularly if there are any technical or specialist elements.
3.  Pull together a first working draft.
4.  Organise an initial review for appraisal and comment.
5.  Refine the document to give final honed responses.
6.  Final check and sign off.

The actual writing of the document needs to consider the tone, style and language to be used.  Some organisations will be explicit in the brand and style of bids, others will leave it to the discretion of bid owners.    Whatever    the    situation    is    within    your organisation make sure that there is a clear story being told throughout the bid.

Developing a clear story means there is:

*   One sentence summing up why the client should choose the organisation.
*   A clear statement about what differentiates the organisation from the competition.
*   A set of answers that demonstrate why the organisation is the logical choice.
*   Something which can be translated into the pitch presentation to give consistency.

**Checklist:**

- *Make sure you adopt the six-step process when it comes to writing the bid.*
- *Establish your process for writing the document, taking into account review and sign-off gateways.*
- *Develop your bid story upfront and include within your answers.*

## 22    Writing the document

Once the invitation to tender has been received, the focus needs to turn to the written document. This means looking at the most effective way of developing and structuring the responses and identifying the value proposition which will differentiate from the competition and resonate with the client.

Ensure someone takes responsibility for reviewing the questions being asked and identify individuals to respond. In a major bid this is often the bid leader. This may mean that more than one person is working on a specific bid; it could be two different technical inputs are required or it could be a technical response is required and marketing need to provide the supporting evidence to illustrate the responses. Whatever the input, ensure someone is collating the responses and then editing so that the style and tone is consistent. For example: is it being written in the third person or using a more informal approach (we, us, you). Also check that numbering and bullets are consistently used, and that the value propositions run throughout each section.

Most importantly make sure the bid demonstrates benefits and not features. Keep sentences short and concise; use active verbs to make an impact; and provide evidence through facts and stats to support statements.

The bid leader needs to provide clarity over the responses required and holding a kick-off meeting to outline the overall opportunity, the value proposition and the schedule of timings is naturally the most effective way of doing this.

**Checklist:**

- *Have a set of clear value propositions fully formulated and agreed before writing the responses.*
- *Use a kick off meeting to share information on the value proposition and schedule of timings with all involved to ensure common understanding and universal agreement.*
- *Create a quick check-list on how to write bids so that there is consistency.*

# 23    Summarising the bid in one page

The big question is: can you sum up the bid on one page? If you can't then the bid theme isn't coherent or the offering is to complex to be easily understood.

Summarising the bid is important, however there is no single way of approaching it as the options are endless.

For example some organisations prefer to use a straight-forward text-based approach, clearly laying out the offering and the advantages so the client can see how the offering feeds into the benefits.

Others use a more elaborate visual-text approach; using single words rather than long bodies of text. These can be single words that illustrate  the differentiators and benefits; others  use  word clouds or tags to create an essence of their bid.

Another option is to have an image based summary.  This may be a flow chart or water-fall of information which lets the client pictorially  see  the  offering.  Alternatively  it  may  be  a roadmap illustrating the offering, journeys and benefits.

Whatever option is used it needs to be part of the bid suite so that it does not appear as an after-thought or adjunct.

**Checklist:**

- *Can you summarise the bid offering onto one page? If not re-visit the bid to simplify or clarify the real value proposition.*
- *Decide which medium and approach is most appropriate to your clients and the procurement specifications.*
- *Remember to use it again in the client presentation for consistency and maximum impact.*

# Prepare for client presentations

Client presentations are the ideal opportunity to make your bid come alive. They give an opportunity to show a joined-up team, passionate about the work and knowledgeable about the practicalities of delivery and implementation.

For this reason the owner of the bid needs to make sure the team is the right one, that the content continues and supports the written submission and that there is a preparation schedule, including a dry-run.

Selecting the right team is key. In an ideal world selecting the right team to present should be easy; however for most it is a juggling act to see whose schedule allows them to be available for the presentation and the rehearsals; who has the right level of knowledge and is comfortable presenting to clients. There also needs to have thought given to capability as well as current performance. After all a shy or inexperienced presenter can be coached for the client presentation so that they become a valuable team member.

Ensuring the presentation continues the bid themes is essential. Weaving the themes into visual, aural and supporting collateral needs to be carefully done. The presentation is the opportunity for the themes to come alive with examples and previous experiences. Remember to break the presentation down into sections to help ensure the team is seen as cohesive and joined up and not dominated by a single person. Ensure the team are prepped and drilled so that they are aware of the overall bid as well as their own part.

Reherse, reherse, reherse again. The more practice the team has, the more comfortable and familiar they will be with presenting the bid solution. Vary the format of the meetings so that different elements are considered. Think about physical presentation, skills, projection, stance and tone. Use senior people or external experts to act as clients and review the performance, record and watch back to critique. All of these give valuable insights into how the team can improve.

**Checklist:**

- *Choose the people who will help form a strong team; be selective and don't be tempted to go for a cast of thousands.*
- *Make sure the bid themes are carefully interwoven into the presentation and bring the bid solution alive for the client.*
- *Look at the schedule and build in team rehearsals. Think about how these will be most effective, ie external reviewer, pseudo-client or peer review.*

# 25     Considering external bid support

It is rare to find a Director responsible for bids who has constant access to instantly available proposal team members and resources. Most are playing a continual juggling game between the opportunities the organisation wants to pursue and the resources available to support.

Depending on the budget available and the time constraints of major bids, the Director may look at buying in external support to help deliver the proposal.

Typically the types of external bid support bought in are:
- Bid writers
- Independent reviewers
- Bid managers
- Bid or pitch trainers

**Bid writers**
Using external bid writers is helpful when there is either a need for additional resource within the team or there is a 'must win' priority proposal that requires a writer who can create compelling value propositions. Bid writers are usually bought in to work on crafting the words within the proposal. Whether they work on-site or remotely they will need to have a clear understanding of the company's key messages and its proposal language.

If you are going to use external writers, consider creating proposal writing guidelines for external writers, similar to the corporate brand guidelines given out to marketing suppliers. Ensure the bid writers know where information sits within your bid resource library so that they don't waste time fruitlessly searching for information that is readily available.

It is also worth considering your bid security. If the writer is working remotely then look at how information is being shared. When you think about how valuable your bids are (in terms of winning and securing work), it is important to think how the information should be protected. Options include secure sites for document transfer and a non-reliance on emails or unencrypted memory sticks.

Proposal writers are usually employed on a day basis or on short-term fixed contracts and can provide a valuable back-up resource.

**Independent reviewer**
The independent reviewer has the joint responsibility of acting as the 'pseudo-client' and as the bid editor. They are usually experienced in dealing with Directors and Board level executives who believe not only that they have all the answers, but that there is never a need for a work count.

To ensure the independent reviewer is able to be an effective member of the client team, it is helpful if they are included at the bid kick-off, that way they have all of the background to the bid decisions rather than having to try and be brought up to speed part-way through.

Independent reviewers are usually brought in to review the value propositions, edit the content and advise on the final documentation. They provide a valuable sense-check for the Director, giving a fresh perspective on how compelling the value propositions appear, whether the wording is suitably crisp and action-orientated, and whether the display is visually easy to follow and understand.

The advantage of having an external independent reviewer is that any constructive criticism, especially to senior members, is delivered with authority by a proposal expert, rather than from someone internally.

**Bid manager**

Bid managers are usually brought in when an organisation has a major or complex tender and has a team whose skill is writing based rather than proposal management or strategic advice.

Bid managers act in a project management role, they plan, manage and coordinate the different stakeholder groups to produce the final proposal in a timely manner.

The benefit of a bid manager is that they bring their experience of handling complex tender submissions, dealing with differing personalities and the ability to work to tight deadlines.

**Bid or pitch trainers**

Bid or pitch trainers can be extremely helpful when it comes to client pitches and presentations. They provide the expertise of bringing together a disparate team so that they appear as a united group. The trainer will often also work on a one-to-one basis, helping individuals develop and hone their own personal presentation skills.

The trainer will usually be brought in after the document has been submitted and the client team know the organisation has been shortlisted.

The benefit the trainer brings to the business is one of training expertise and time to be able to work with the client presentation team to get the best from them.

**Checklist:**

- *Make sure you provide adequate time to outline the company's approach and processes so that you get the most from your external suppliers.*
- *Consider the confidentiality and security of content and information around your bid when using external suppliers.*
- *Review and rate supplier performance so that you address small issues in a timely manner, and allow them to amend before working on the next proposal.*
- *Provide clear specifications and timescales so that suppliers know when they are expected to deliver.*

 # Templates and bid designers

To create consistently high-quality bids which can be replicated, it is a good idea to have a series of bid templates. These may be for use by the bid team or for specialist bid document designers.

The advantage of a bid document designer is that they can be used when the bid requires something other than the standard bid template or when there is not enough internal resource to cover the workload.

To ensure that the bid document designers adhere to the company branding, they need to have an introduction to the corporate brand guidelines, together with any restrictions over palette colours, styles of imagery and graphics, preferred layouts and constraints of the final bid document.

Using an external bid document designer is a valuable support for the Director responsible for bids, however it is always worth checking technology compatibility before work commences on the document. There is nothing more frustrating than finding a typo in the text just before sending to print, and discovering that it is impossible to amend in-house.

If the team is too stretched or inexperienced then having occasional external support can provide a work-around solution on must-win opportunities.

**Checklist:**

- *Ensure you have templates that are high-quality and of a professional standard.*
- *Have templates that are usable by the organisation.*
- *If you use bid document designers, provide comprehensive user-friendly bid style guidelines which can be given to suppliers before they start work.*

 **Case study: Why a bid/no bid delivers value**

A professional services firm was using its bid teams to focus on multiple lower-value bids at the expense of the larger opportunities.

The firm had a series of lower-value bids with key clients which needed quick turnaround on to ensure qualification for next stage. However the firm's bid team had to do this at the expense of larger value bids for unknown targets.

The firm realised that it needed a bid/no bid process to prevent the firm from missing out on larger opportunities because of smaller bids with familiar clients.

The bid/no bid process had to take into account client status, value of bid, probability of winning, resources required and fit of offering. This was achieved by adopting a balanced scorecard approach. This allowed bids to be prioritised and ranked by the business before the bid team began work.

The result was the business was able to give the bid team specific opportunities. By working together the client facing teams were able to evaluate the must-win bids which were strategically important for the firm. This meant the firm had a bid team that was able to concentrate on winning the bids that the firm strategically required.

 **Client Review**

"The bid doesn't end, it becomes the working relationship with the client. This means the bid team needs to maintain contact."

# 27     Ask for feedback

Any bid should always be followed up with a formal request for feedback, regardless of whether it is a win or a loss. This information is a valuable insight into a client's buying decision and should be considered when bidding for more work.

The level and degree of feedback from clients will vary greatly from simple statements such as price or capability through to well-crafted critiques which expand upon areas of differentiation and key areas of persuasion.

All feedback should be collated centrally and reviewed so that the bid team can view trends appearing in the feedback.

**Checklist:**

- *Feedback is a vital piece of client insight particularly when preparing for the next bid.*
- *Integrate the process for requesting feedback into the overall bid process.*
- *Share feedback with the other client facing teams.*
- *Consider how and where client feedback will be held so that it is accessible.*
- *Decide how the feedback can be translated into valuable lessons learnt for subsequent bids.*

# 28     Conduct a debrief on a large bid

Whether it is a win or a loss, always carry out a full debrief on a large bid. It is a valuable source of information, both on recognising what went well and what worked for the client, but also for providing lessons learnt on what could be improved for future bids.

The bid leader should take responsibility for organising, facilitating and sharing the outputs of the debrief. Others who should attend are the relevant bid team members, operational staff and client facing account managers, Directors or Partners.

The type of questions to consider within a debrief are:
- What went well
- Why was it seen as valuable to the client
- What aspects underperformed

Take the lessons learnt and look at how existing processes, practices and resources would need to be changed so that the same mistakes or errors are not replicated in future bids.

**Checklist:**

- *Use the outputs from the bid debrief to examine current bid processes in order to continually improve.*
- *Set up a bid debrief process.*
- *Adopt a standard approach to a bid debrief so that results can be compared to identify any underlying trends.*
- *Share lessons learnt with client facing teams.*

# 29    Case studies and testimonials

One very effective way of demonstrating your understanding of client and sector issues is the judicious use of case studies and testimonials.

Before work begins on creating case studies it is worth thinking about the four key considerations:
- Who should you use
- Where will you use them
- How will you use them
- What format should the case studies take

### Who should you use?

Gathering case studies can be time consuming, you therefore want to make sure you are maximising your return on effort. Select clients whose issues are similar to the other targets you are pursuing. Where possible have well-known brands as this will have the halo-effect on your brand. You do not need to limit yourself to only considering current clients; take a look at your historic clients as well when you are drawing up your shortlist.

### Where will you use them?

Case study content is multi-purpose. It can be used to support a number of marketing and business development functions. Case studies are a useful addition to the company website, supporting media pieces, including within proposals and featuring in newsletters and mailings.  Re-purpose the core content so that it can be used in multiple places.

## How will you use them?

Case studies are powerful advocates for you; however it is not just the end case study which has the value.  By building the case study into the client review process it both gives you the opportunity to positively re-inforce the work or products provided and to understand the real benefits the client has realised.  Using a script means that the content for a case study can easily be incorporated into a meeting without the need for additional meetings.

## What format should the case studies take?

There are a number of options around the format of case studies; written A4 pages are the usual style employed by most companies.  However there is no reason why a number of different styles should not be used.  Other formats can include written interviews with the client using a question and answer format, videos of a client interview, visual infographics and montages of sound-bytes from the client team and your own organisation.

Whatever format you decide to go with, it is important when compiling case studies that they clearly show:
- What was the issue being faced by the client?
- How did your organisation identify and deliver an effective solution?
- What hurdles (ie process/culture/resourcing) did you have to overcome?
- What was the end result for the client?
- How did this benefit their organisation?

By using these questions as a script, the case studies should clearly show how the organisation effectively works with clients to solve their problems.

Testimonials provide a similar rich example. Again these can be included as part of the final or annual client review. Usually these will be from recent contracts, however once again it is possible to approach historic clients, particularly if they are an influential brand or key player in the sector.

**Check list:**

- *Work through the four key considerations before you begin compiling the case studies.*
- *Create a standard script, regardless of the format you intend to use, so that information is collected in a clear methodical way and valuable information is not missed.*
- *Avoid listing the features as this adds no value. Similarly do not be tempted to list out what you provided step-by-step as these will not gain traction with a client.*
- *Ensure your case studies demonstrate the value and benefits of the solutions provided.*

# 30     Assess the bids you turned down

Analysis of the bids which you didn't pursue is a valuable insight. Try to establish if there are trends in the findings. Consider whether you were repeatedly asked to bid for work which was unattractive or unprofitable. Did limited bid team resource availability prevent you being able to bid, and was this due to lack of holiday cover or an ongoing issue? Were the companies asking you to bid not your target clients?

If the company is being asked to bid for unattractive work or the companies are not your targets then the bid team need to share the findings with the wider organisation. It would appear that companies are under the impression that you want to provide these services and work with them. Look at all your channels; are they consistent and harmonious with what the company wants to provide and be seen to be providing?

If there is a resourcing issue then the Director responsible needs to identify whether it can be resolved through working more effectively or if additional resources are required at certain peak times.

**Check list:**

- *Analyse the bids and determine the root cause for non-pursuit.*
- *Share the findings with the wider client facing team to ensure mixed messages aren't being given to the market.*
- *Consider most effective resource planning and*

*allocation (including external support) if prime opportunities are not being pursued.*

 ## Case study: The value of pitch training

A construction organisation had an inexperienced team for pitches and client presentations. This meant they were under-confident and therefore underperforming when it came to the final bid selection.

The issue was that the Operations team were involved with the technical aspects of the bid, however they were not given any preparation for the client pitches and presentations. This was particularly the case when they were co-presenting with the Sales team. The result was the team came across as fractured and uncoordinated in the client presentation.

To resolve the issue the company decided to create a tailored pitch and presentation training programme that both provided experience to the Operations team, but also gave a structured approach for the Operations and Sales teams to work effectively together. This included a four step pitch process that included everyone involved with the presentation.

Through the training programme, the Operations and Sales teams became more familiar with the other's strengths and knowledge, which meant that working on bids became more effective. The result was a cohesive team that consistently delivered an effective client presentation. There were also specific training sessions on how to present to a client.

30 ways to win a bid

 **... and finally**

Whatever bids your company produces, whatever your bid approach and ethos, the key is to remember that the bid is only part of the overall client opportunity.

Bids should never be seen in isolation; they are an integral part of the client-facing team. This means whether you are labelled marketing, business development, sales or bids you still have a role to play in creating winning bids.

To create winning bids the organisation needs to recognise this sentiment and support it with the five-tenements of client-centric teams. This ensures there is client-centricity across all of the client facing teams so that bids is an integral part of the work winning spectrum.

By having this firm foundation the organisation is then able to review their current performance within each stage of the bid life cycle.

By reviewing your performance and identifying areas for improvement, the organisation will be able to selectively target must-have wins, convert low conversation rates and look to increase the number of bids that it successfully wins.

By working through the 30 steps, your organisation should be well placed to be winning more bids and having a successful bid team.

www.ingramcontent.com/pod-product-compliance
Lightning Source LLC
Chambersburg PA
CBHW070106210526
45170CB00013B/773